The Grimoire of Grimalkin
Sascha Aurora Akhtar

But, as touching this Grimmalkin, I take rather to be an hagat or a witch than a cat, for witches have gone often in that likeness and therof hath com the proverb, as true as common, that a cat hath nine lives, that is to say, a witch may take on her a cats body nine times.
   William Baldwin, *Beware the Cat* (1570)

PREFACE Ágnes Lehóczky   ix

movement I

    IMMERITO MEO   5
    URBAN OJOURN   7
    ENUEG   11
    MARASMUS   14
    LIVERISH   23
    CATHEXIS 1:1   26
    CATHEXIS 2:1   28
    CATHEXIS 2:2   32
    TRIBUNAL   33
    SIRVENTE MOT   34
    SUBFUSC   37
    SOEUR   38
    FRÈRE   39

caesura

    AMIDST   43
    WHAT A RUCKUS   44
    PHYSIX   45
    FOUL PLAY   47
    SABLE POEM   49

movement II

    LA PEINTURE   55
    EASTERN EUROPEAN EGRESS   56
    ABACUS   61
    STEW & YORKSHIRE PUDDING 63
    BEIGNET   67
    60 BY 120 KM ELLIPSE   71
    VALHALLA   76

AFTERWORD Sascha Aurora Akhtar   81

PREFACE
Ágnes Lehóczky

With its translingual alchemy, Sascha Aurora Akhtar's extraordinary spellbook weaves a liminal space that's both familiar and unsettling. It's a politicised public square charged with both private intimacy and magical realism, an idiosyncratic, idiomatic world that is both historical and futuristic.

This 'retro-futuristic' realm in relentless metamorphosis plays with time, oscillating between a confusing past and a dreaded future, all within a grotesquely realistic present. The book rewrites the past in an old tongue, mocking the dead and poking fun at outdated dialectics of love. It constantly name-drops figures (are they friends or foes?) like Gogol and Michael Gizzi, while hinting at others like Borges and Bulgakov.

It also yearns for a new political language, a tongue we haven't grasped yet. It's both deconstruction (logoclasm) and construction (language-building). This foully fair and playful in-between space, dictated by a fierce feminist, a trickster figure (homo ludens), is written in commands and governed by ever-shifting rules. This unreliable narrator, sometimes a terrifying cat, sometimes a polyglot scholar, sometimes a bumbling 'idiot', speaks the truth in tongues, in an idiolect that is both grotesque and unforgiving.

Despite the absurdity, the 'idiot's truth' is undeniable. We must listen closely to this paradoxical meta-book, this radically provocative love letter written 'in a language of love / baked into a brie / of hate already cold / in a box on the bus / from Hades'.

The Grimoire of Grimalkin

movement I

IMMERITO MEO

An   erratic locale
       in which to sell myself
       to Asiatic emu farmers
&

   Visigoths

         Tell me the wind

   has wound

its way through

      my
         carte
            blanche

I am not

an erosion of semi-soft
Appalachian cheese rind

muck-raker you

      a muck-raker

      till the dénouement
of the tale
      unravelled

in a language of love
baked into a brié
of hate already cold
in a box on the bus
from Hades

I talk of null
        & flavourful
        trysts

with acquaintances,
belongings that belong

to no-one.

Bearer of chance
my criminal propensities
must pay for

to please

        me/you

            kill it off

                barely contained

in this space, in this time.

Lend me a glen
for every pretty girl
out for the night
during the day
la langoustine est morte et
la bouche quand elle parle
dit: *au moment du sommeil
nous ecrivons dans le caboose*

                d'amour pres de la mer.

URBAN SOJOURN

I

She calls severance, fatal
altruism won't help now

Bedded a black wager, won
wined & dined till the cows came home

Let them fall where they may, the cows
like cursed hair off a fallow baroness

My restraint comes like a constipate
trying to pass a bowel movement.

Oui, oui j'entends
Why do you bellow?
      Why do you blush so?

In the woods
hunters sit & long for the mark
to make them men.

Smooth the smell of gunpowder
sweeter than you who puts the dog out,

    yanks him back in

When it becomes fun, cruel actor
committing this felony with an amiable smile

Patting his head good boy, good boy
good milk turns sour in your wake.

A single fluke worm
assiduously burrowing
    sticks his head out

An unwitting mouth bites it in half;
neither one knows what happens next

II

I saw a portal into the future
on the cobblestones
    exchanged saliva

Brain dipped in ink
stamps over, over & over
your name.

With cigarette fingers
roam these dark streets dressed
in case I meet el Diablo

Look up everywhere
there are crows
perched on the fingertips of trees, solemn
conference, realm of senses
that lies where, who knows.

Vermouth in a tall glass, white
sheet taut clutched over head, crave
the dawn
    crystals crack in nose, liver
laments at the tenacity of the unexpected

to have its way

whilst in feather boas, I dance

the ice

You runnin' away from home?
want to put your shoes under my bed
your coat in my closet?

  & I think
    why
      the fuck not
        why the fuck
not?

ENUEG

I

Keel over & die

>Nothing will happen
>no-one will frame it
>for posterity, regress
>a summons keen & crisp
>to get your attention, fraternise
>with the neighbours; that old woman
>named Dodo in the red barn.
>
>A bat fried on the electric heater
>starts to stink up the place
>
>Can you hear it? It's bliss.
>
>Egalité sounds like a burp
>I am here, nothing clicks
>but my clackity click fingers, lick
>toes try to drink flesh stop me
>
>if you've heard, the gruesome display bride
>with a bullet-hole
>>through the centre of her head.
>
>Put it on the death-wall, where else can it go?

In avoiding the pull of gravity

>there are only two possibilities: A or B
>*don't know* is not an answer, *must go*
>not an answer, too slow
>not an answer, down low circumstance
>>denies itself, the crick in your back
>>unwinds itself, landing you in the fray.

A Spanish temple on a warm day accounts for all of it.

You seek out this travesty
gain indecision for your pains
the worst of all evils on display, cool & creamy
summertime pie advertised
as all it's meant to be

They do not deliver,
            it cannot be had

the disdain for the act
must be paid out in full.

It's the only way we'll get rid of them.

Go home, go home I tell you
                There is nothing to see here
                                but yourselves.

II

I landed on the island,
the island was grey.

My boots filled with chips
faster than that wink
of that eye I always hear about.

Some people can't you know, wink

They try & try, like whistling like
whooping, like wanking, like
waiting, like winning. Like
writing, like wailing; seasickness
I surmise it was whilst on land
& motion sickness whilst standing
quite, quite still.

Collude with the day,
it has made provisions.
Basking in air shine I grasp for it

                    & it grasps back for me.

MARASMUS

After O. Mirbeau

I

& in this room
is a geriatric
in a wheelchair
that she has sex with, then leaves
his body in another room
where the dead man & girlfriend
      sleep
   girlfriend moans
   dead man asks her
tenderly
   if she's okay.

Girl feels the bile
rise
 in her mouth

Back
Beat
a hasty retreat.

There is a moment
    between deaths
when you meet
    the homunculus
& he tells
  you all your secrets.

This is not one
   of those times
all is not well
   & ordained
      this is a time

when all
　are fraught
with Obsession
　　　Upon my wit,
　　　　　I have not an ounce
more to give
　　　　my obsession.

II

    She loves him
            this dead man
        girlfriend tells
     stories in French
   subtitled in Vietnamese
   she sees none of it
      only eyes
burgeoning into bloom
like lettuce on the streets
         in November
  & savage nosebleeds
              with no end
       pouring
    onto the pavement
  side   skip
        step   miss
  umbrellas collide
             unless
you raise
  one higher than the liar
  who escapes by telling
    one truth.

III

We roam the wilds
unto no end
    if we should get lost
No one
    shall find us
I promise
  just keep
walking
 lift the trees
upon your shoulders
    show the eaves
      your laughter
        just walk with me a while.

IV

    & in this deciduous well
we fall prey to freebooters
& magi of make-believe,
who take pleasure in sowing
us like arable land in this dwelling

of hindsight.

Suggest another season.

Buy some time with all that trust
you have in your brother's keeper.

    v

Garbage & entrails
    follow
  me like flies
some would say
she is possessed
  by another
some

would say anything
to make a quick buck
    fuck
shit out
  of lacrima.

The most voracious don
she ever did try
    to resist
smarting at the seams
of treason
    &
      sclerous
will to control
the comma,
the period,
the cock.

VI

    Sullen, the processional
cracks its whip
      into the salt mines
   we climb
Shiftless
   wake of living exile

She beseeches
   the priest
to hear her confess
from behind
   the wailing vault
he is reading
a requiescat
   for the dead man
who still roams

        Spending
his seed for salvation
he thinks
he will be forgiven.

The dead man is my father

Hear me now
& I will forever hold you
with contempt.

VII

His breath blows
like a   scirocco
through my blood
girlfriend rolls her eyes
      succumbs
  to the narcolepsy
  bestowed upon her
  petaloid lips shut
     scarlet
     & sound
  the dead man
     claws
     clutches
  at his cage
        the girl stands there
watching
slowly   raising
        one
       hand
     as if to dance
he snarls & shivers
        she runs the tip
of her tongue
     along the cold
steel bars
tasting
  his
     sweat

Please help me.

VIII

Gallstones & haemorrhoids beleaguer
my physical being, in the bestiary
there are thorny rose bushes that provide
some relief from the pleasure I take
in your enjoyment of my torment.

In frosty nooks I conceal myself
from the men in sombreros
& serapes.

She hears his voice talk
through the rabbit holes
in the field & replies

Give me pain.

LIVERISH

Get you home, you merry lads: Tell your mammies & your dads,
& all those that news desire, How you saw a walking fire
Babes as soon as they can lisp, Used to call me Will-y-wisp
If that you but weary be, It is sport alone for me.
Away: unto your houses go, & I'll be laughing, Ho, ho, ho!
      Will-o'-the-Wisp, Old English rhyme

  I

Weigh the tops
of tattletale grey lines scratched
under my eyes, against the tide
& oh you'll get such a drubbin'
when your father gets home
promise to be nothing of the sort.

Surgeon
  under oath sews lightly
            with black thread up
                    shreds of
                        remorse
                        he appears
     a taipo in thorns
under the influence
  of a demiurge
  we have moved
the minds
  of miracles
    an ignis fatuus
you relieve nothing
    with   rout it up
       for further avowals
  defaming
    the corposant
      of this battered legion

   entitled
    to fight
for the indiscretions
   against its houri
grant common carnal knowledge
to all *umbrae ex mos moris laesum*

Vum! This will-o'-the-wisp
hangs around my ears
           loik a snake

               coruscating
               vulgarly

all its shallow
depths.

II

    the corpus is prepared as
    corpus delicti, swanny
    for your trespass
    I will give you
    in dainty Italian glass
    my guts as gelato
    & cambric tea
    poured from steaming
    silverware, with hemlock
    for cream & teeth
    ground into sugar

You, of the blue in red
   eft soons will be gelt.

CATHEXIS 1:1

Summonare, agente con Diable
summoneo l'arbre de cyprés
stationnaire. Summonare
summoneo meus argentum
dentes effulsi dans la boue
levate! les rides
sur mon front
summonare ha summonare ha summonare

On a summer's day, a sundowner slays
his friend the stinkbug
ah you malefic member
ah you maraud abroad
ah mayhem merry merry
doth make summoner
summon me, some are stars
some are other
mollusks.

A tiny callipygian char, smoking
a chibouk in the mosque
will do nicely & ven we dance
the chaconne be sure it will be remembered not
pro bono cut a line, cut a lust off
like a limb of Giacometti in a giggle boat
ghost in the gibbet hole why ghost
in the crinoline.

Chaw roast, conifer toast
fit for sin to shrive in
gewgaws & gill slits
on a whim yet ho! sour
soubrette no need to
grease your muffin tin
with cerumen, chancre or chancroid

je tu? je tu? je et tu?

Hispid claw, angels gawk & graze
in dismay holy shits
come what may
grace amazing, jugs of camphor
vurds flail, giaours ail at the seams
of contusion sortilege in praxis
or sodomy, unmistakable.

Clew of Theseus sedated from the hip
bilabial trip, crypt cringe
biggity biggity, not to be outdone
that bitch inflection, shoot the tube
summonare! sorcier! billabong!
all in one.

Cut-throat heresy hinges
hypopnea hinges ectoplasm
hinges, hinge on hinges hinge
on everything hinged on one
nostrum bigos for supper none
succotash gin larder in a barouche
Anastasia! rides for the debridement
Oh sweet morphine debouchure
with Gideons & Gorgons she
go-no-go esta von solo unreposed
progenitor of Spoonerisms & other

frangible mercenaries.

CATHEXIS 2:1

Esta con dios
eras enclaved in endbrain,
bowl a rope, smote
on the entresol of hate
& concupiscence for embryos
in toboggans slayed in jars of
regulus regulus
fossil slumgullion awaits wicked
catsup way waste, a perfectly good
imbroglio.

Berate, beat a wake 'em, snake 'em
the journeyman knows
the cataclysm concedes to deviate
anon I come

On smazy rimmed spectacles
chalix of Frangelika & bad taste in mouth
aura unhand the swine, he's all not quite
divine three pronged shift, lakes haemorrhage
slumber hangs a rose over the cobblestones
to mark the secrecy of this hour.

Camarilla of dastardly mutts ensconced
faithfully, you be wary conceal
visage, folds into prayer prostate
the gland not related to anile infractions
of veni vidi vici, caramel supine
languor mould on haggis delicious
votto soce blue me
you are the enantiomorph, I the ante.

Singe the shoe she crows
enceinte who who who
gesture in the gulch falls short
of the bravest gross echanté
le plaisir est toujours à moi.

A case of mismanaged
idée fixeé in the gallows bellows
on bellows, bellow on Bella
the sage revives her ridden hatch
gets goitre, got saunter up
to the minx & ask her a
favour for old times.

Sat on a mat his wife could eat no
& that was bother! bother!
bother! Grind the stones to sand
& fill with ambergris the livid cheeks
surprise no other but you,
scab the wrist, braid the suture.

a loving embrace spits ambeer
on more of the same
& grist & grits
& free grub for all
        Eh Effendi!
Effendi the gall, the knock-
me-down-with-a-feather you
employ, Effendi the executrix
consumes your shine she sells
crooks her lithium smile
gracile child of a child of a,
you are manqué,
gonzo Rhadamanthus!

Hold up the bloodstained sheet
to her materfamilias who
would have taught it so-&-such
& so many agile rows, docile
caboodles & caboodles of
foreskins laid to wage a sobriquet
quiet sorbet of mange & misery
commensurate with lathe return no

request no, balk at the
stakes & stones will speak
volumes to you who grates,
gawks, regurgitates at green landfills.

William my son, father my budgerie
still lives, equate nothing
with frugal hegemony too late it's never
well I never! Commiserate amour
no not yeasty cakes ale brewed
by the breath of shy lionesses
hot for the pride bites
its own head & we laugh it off
nudge, nudge nefarious purpose
screened into place, forfeit
at the angle of yaw
see all the way through
to the mist & catarrh.

Gilded gates awaken Eros flown
the coop born to swoop off talipots
in Thatta, tender icicles
a shoe-in at the races, bet your bottom
collar a codge of miserable
oboe players will befriend

the man-o'-war.
Imogen lays awake planning
the feint parry thrust
of the ne'er-do-well.

To do a number with you
in the throes of egregious limp ice-cream
cones for a spell manic
aspen seeds fill my coat with nap
hoodwink a dinky predicate factor
in factor out, a genus remote

indication crumb undone
Bella accrues the gain lofty
shiny fourchettes for the groom
to stab his fingers in a game
on the kitchen table
only an oblong converges
& we give it nothing

tangible.

CATHEXIS 2:2

Shoe a slumber
await shoe a
suffocate burgess
not too late for you
in cowlick & cowls
your presence at the throne
singe the, singe the
beginning of the end
like wax & a frozen
fondue fantasy philanders
at the windy tower.

immersion not emulsion
constantinople & a gerbil
holding hands & whiskers.

TRIBUNAL

Fortune arrives wedded by the bell
I cannot calm her down, she screams
of an abscess in her gums.
I tell her to sit on the bench,
& drink some tea; my friend has engaged
the rain to play at his funeral, he says
not to worry, the band will be along shortly.

In the basket are june bugs
waiting to pounce on picnickers, hungry
for egg salad sandwiches & pickled herring.
A congress of dervishes is gathering
under the silver birches whilst bankers die
of botulism in the park.

Overhead in the elm tree, one
scarlet tanager starts to sing, announcing
a chopine race, the wizened organ grinder lurches
a scherzo, tap-dancing on the green
baring his gums in a smile leaking
at the sky.

A plastic hand reaches
out of the perambulator & looks at me
askance. I have no milk, so I ask
the vegetarian cineaste next to me
Does he have any? Mother runs over
with a bag of durians & a chocolate
cigar, gives us a dirty look
& pops out her breast, veined
like Stilton
    & I wonder
    perhaps breasts
        do become cheese after a time.

SIRVENTE MOT

Nary the word prompts
the hegira of thought,
gotta get got while the going's good

A substrate of jejune fiends looking
for act or diction arms akimbo stand
as an obstruction

This domicile of dearth
& good hope cannot be deserted
so easily; immurement at the very least

Might please the merry flock, basking
in the misericord for the interim, moving
away from the point of no recovery I tread

The mill meekly milking mounds of mellifluent
colicky infrahumans for that gram
of gab to fill the yawning gape only
to rebound like a jacaranda ball to my jaw.

I am Sisyphus
         & these words are the boulder, my effort
my life-warrant.

A last-ditch derring-do might release
the rubber man but all I see are
cartoons in cartouches when I close my eyes

To breathe is not a good thing, it reprieves
when reprieval is not sought after. I deign, I drug,
I dose mosso in a free & facile fission

I have met the Demiurge
& he is a pretty sight
for eyes sore from photophobia
forced to see the sleight of hand
that tugs at the ballast
of the boor, & you do know glume: one of the two chaffy
basal bracts of a grass spikelet.

When would an exclamation be a question too?
So this, this interrobang
I have never laid a hand on could be used

Are you quite sure about this? It's not just a ploy
to get me to join your seraglio
spanning the galaxy of lingual acrobatics.

There is no need, I assure you
for the flagellation of my wit your eyes
hold the promise of cannot come
at a better time.

We can estivate in the hyponasty
of the li pai tien , fashion an intarsia
on my nates with nothing more
than a bodkin &
               lekvar to soothe the rawness.

Away from the ruck, two quarks of a hadron
two glumes of a grass spikelet figures
in a grisaille made by the laureate's daughter
parlour games on the parquet,
               dinner with Scaramouch
               & his schipperke.

You the nostrum & I the piolet.

Don't presume to prescind
from such jinks, I told you I had nothing
to say; a tall pig made smaller
than the pince-nez perched

on the nose of a pissant & ...
I am spent. Nowhere to chasse
but the charnel house, no place to glissade

But the gauntlet, abominations surfeit.
I am doomed to be kept awake
by the rhonchus from your lungs

Ah I could make a jink here but apostates too
must make amends, scratch my scarious flesh
a little while longer, I can prevaricate no more.

Idiot or idiolect who can tell?

SUBFUSC

After Bernadette Mayer

Nothing is sharp at six a.m.
but the blinding sting
of the sunrise in the irises
    Jonathan Sajda

        Doctor the morphine hurts me.
Daughter the morphémès must be divided into dulcets packaged
    into tidy wads of embolalia for the grimus
comes to wait at the foot of my head
a little while longer
        Doctor I am petrified
of the maquette in the almira, dodger
desist I am dizzy desirous of perpetual langweile
        Wearing my wig of bluebells
I shake my musty arms at. I must eke
out this façade of nervous nurses & dalmatian wards
grown feral in denominations of ten
swollen tangos & seven tangerines insistent
wille zum leben decides to take me for a constitutional
amongst the eaves of thought negative
g-force makes me retch. The Ace of Knaves
is uncovered from amongst the shrubbery. A dubious
pleasure this anabolic frolic from the start
heigh-ho
these guys are
      end of mission.

Following on all fours, tails of the unexpected
not to you, but to your incision, a few
pennies chinkling change left
over in case the élan returns ergo
I cannot complain drambuie
I must confess on the brink
of penury to indulge in. Nothing short of
fabulous.

SOEUR

Steal criminy steal from the frogs seal
thunder into a talisman around your neck ward

off the compassion of your brother
concealed in storm clouds

under the bed. Don a basque
made of a pirate's flag & keep his severed

hand between your legs. Bury the bassinet make
haste a song simple la la coryphée in pink

tonight decides to kill the prima donna. Lays low
like a shark basking in the water spring

at the drop of my hat, its all wet now
naked best for a scramble in the bramble ripped

clean through my farthingale muddy
feet bereft of buskins. Await the concessionary

kiss & pray for tongues & top hats
pater faitour nein smooth your lambchops

love of me dead you see me as fine puff pastry
lick each finger lovingly. Trees speed by colours

change from spring to fall winter summer I sigh

                Sigh

                the last bastion of relief not in sight

FRÈRE

He waits in the forest to batfowl
little lasses in dolmans

To have his way with while in dreams
her silent shadow watches

the Rape of Lucrece
her mistress, happen to her

Bites his fingernails to the quick buries
himself in books to conceal from prying

Eyes his looming alopecia
chomp chomp on choice cuts & drippings

Dipped in white bread, white flesh spilling
forth in garters. He keeps her lactating

Pins basket stars behind glass.

The greatest trick of all

                performed with a wink:

                            je n'existe pas.

caesura

AMIDST

Thank you for the poetry books
to line my walls with superstitio
rides in bubbles, astride my brain

The lot of old worlders
& new, shiny people
call it ignorance of the laws

Of nature, irrational belief
in magic or chance, a complete erosion
of the person in one conviction

Rhetorical questions aside, you believe
in the mirror & what you see
the unseen does not exist

There is no world other than this
Galileo imprisoned for advancing
heliocentricity, it was you wasn't it

A prophet aspires to dull revulsions
& we yawn & call next. Another spiritual
coup pulled off most elegantly

As heard on the radio
Kill duck before

serving.

WHAT A RUCKUS

After Michael Gizzi

Is there a mouse
in the bowling alley?
Oh my, is there a mouse
in the bedroom? Oh my!

Are there gnats in hats?
Are there shoestrings
in tin cans, are there grey sheep
in the alley lookin' for trouble,
are there rats in my belfry?

Is there bedlam in the pizza
joint? Are there warts on the table?
Is there a single rhyme that doesn't

Are there giants that are
Are there green gables
Is that a poppy in my plate?
Are there knees in the soup

Oh I do hope so because
I really like knees in my soup,
adds to the flavour don'tcha think?

Like Onions.

PHYSIX

Nice a rind &
a rind all around

a small window
in the wall
the size of a small pre-gessoed

canvas I paint
branches without leaves
the shadow of

in the midnight
approaching light
how to revive rice

her hair tied up in a tight
chignon looks like
her neck smiles

Arching an eyebrow
if I say my
& you say my
does it become
ours & we?

Five million years I
slept for, nothing
changed.

A party, a periodic
table, a party, on the
ironing board is a bar,

of elements

Scandium; rare
atomic number 21
protons highly charged
in the centre right next to Ti

occurring widely

Negative electron
dictates this fundamental name

An electron
              is not a hadron.

              I beat the physicist at
              hangman, he beat
              me back with

                      quark.

FOUL PLAY

Sorry stitches saving nine & a half dames
& nits from a fate more dull than dire

Blonde hairs found in clothes, in the carpet
in sheets, on the keyboard even if I knew

Better I'd say it was black magic driving
down something, something salt or snow? An illusion

Of promise & torture surfeit to say nothing
remembers my mind. The language decided

To have enough be the root of sad
all the livelong day cousin

Buttercup & Aunt Amanda party it up
on the verandah & no-one is ever the wiser.

Home for the Disenchanted; read poets. Home
for Ribald & Abusive Personages; read *skald*

Read poet. As Sanctioned By Language.
Don't ask for anything we'll give you

What we can, here's my number
as if he foresees I will need

It, a freshly-bit victim
when the Thirst starts

In the bulges of the brain
an oyster irritated produces

A barroco. I produce
this, this, this; Reade und Weepe

All this time a conspiracy
 it amazes to conceal good poetry
  uncovered
   & there's me thinking it didn't exist.

SABLE POEM

Not so much so no
no not at all
so, goons & grapes parading
like everlasting crêpes folded
at the cornershop with chocolate
& bananas enough to make one wish

One wish one was never
at three thirty-three it appears
like pennies in a wishing well
the continent broke away
& so there are jagged coastlines
in England & Maine

A nervous tic toc-ing, the sound
of a stomach digesting
itself while you lie
in bed with him, all temptress
& seduction glaze wearing off
steadily as if the sleigh rode all

All night bearing gifts for the good
& cancer for the bad & you wonder
about the school of hard knocks
right next to the Chinese bakery
where they won't sell you butter buns
just out of the oven, like Grandma's bread

Just get on the bus & wait for it to take you
places you wanted to go when you bought the ticket
but have changed your mind since
the chambers don't communicate anymore
& this man in a monkey suit continues to gesticulate

Frantically at the electrical pole
but he's not an electrician, so you walk away
come quietly or forever hold your peace
I have a very good reason, only
now there are three. We bought one for the boy
one for the girl, one for the dog

A perfect picture of a picture taken
when things were black-&-white, a shame
to boast about one so young & gormless
there are so many decimated civilizations
makes one wonder really. Do I have a head

or do I just think so
              & is there, is there life on Earth?

Surrender is 9/10ths I hear like lying
awake in bed whilst the person next to you
is sleeping soundly:

> *Your softly snoring silence sleeps away*
> *my dreams.*

movement II

LA PEINTURE

Tristan carnival a bulwark upon
blaze me a laugh á jus meo gravio
where is her head where black
strands each woven pupa around
no face Tristan your walnuts
well so fit sweeny my palm
feel near surface ribs so feel
with finger pronounce each one
madhocks hurly-burly at ad hoc
junction.

    Desiree deliquesce
into politesse armagnac sous vela
vela Titian a young man as
eyebrow brown stare in
to me is more is
makes sound pop sternum
makes sound no dura mater
heard is champagné
on bottom of barouche
scraping slug maze trail
we you follow
to no place nausea.

EASTERN EUROPEAN EGRESS

After Gogol Hutz &
the Whores of the Bordello

Sur tide, casbah delay
sclerosis livid hydrangea

>blossoms at The Corinthian
>maze in the deserts of Arabia
>no romance lost only belly-dancers
>in tents watched by fat fasting men
>smoking sheesham in hookahs
>that look like spaceships
>a gentle prosody, if you stay
>awake all night there is this
>moment a flash where all
>is known the answer is 42.

Oh casbah grant a *takht*
to these daughters

>& velvet cushions
>delicious smoky
>invite laced with
>apheem & gasoline
>the gypsy trance
>in bells & accordions
>preen parade purple
>you wear & smack
>of hope & good will
>speak in your little voice
>prognosticate this
>alleviate that

Casbah your diction

>awaits war-torn
>tirade hours blown
>up no decision reached

viva paranoia

viva dulce musto

viva viva

nada cantata est depravé

Stella burn illumine
graves & contemplate
this, a jet engine longer.

Grimace pulled into
tart ancestral lines

> run amok between eyes
> & eyebags. A spider
> weaves along the edges
> her final defence against
> age & pleasure in pleasure
> taken lightly she eats
> roasted sunflowers

& dandelions

> on crisp leaves & demands
> peach schnapps on demand
> a screeching pain was the only
> announcement we heard
> while the world delighted
> in towns alight with
> the blaze of bombings.

Sure thing I'll lend
you a penny

> for every dollar you spend

on waging vicious
retribution on the wilds
dostustrum furmante
lugallo vivante sum
lay down in the street
they'll drive over you anyway
good thing you're made of rubber.

In your lies, rhinestones
spitting forth as she walks
calando a trail glistering
green & red like silver
snail goo.

Caliginous morning

the ass rides his ass
despite the swamp
      outside his window.

    Overnight the orange tree
    started blooming in lady's
    slippers pert & polite,
    we tried to avoid it
    but we had no luck
    with longing in the
    maze designed on
    the whim of a star
    a silver spoon attached
    to his spine

    it was a joke really
    it was.
    How was I supposed
    to know you wanted
    to
        find a way out.

Obvious is as obvious
does the toothy afternoon

> loves to remind its fallow
> phrases that an ounce of sprat
> is worth two in the lean
> way she was rarefied
> & they knew as much
> pursued by every male
> thirsty for progeny to
> carry his blood-name
> repeat offenders
> all uncalled for
> that was,
> I remember the
> time when Russia was
> one & we were tired
> & yet continued.

There are bastards & there
are buzzards, name your poison

> shrug, shrug, shrieve it off
> like an elegant sprite
> dangling diphthongs
> for sport seems like
> a hobby of sorts
> on your part claiming
> desecrated niceties as
> your own.

Aye beliefe
the high tide

> runs low & we shall
> see all the shrapnel
> washed up on the shore

      of midgeons & molworts
      my able babel fish will allow
      us to understand each
      other even though you
      lay contrariwise to
      Paradiza & I clockwise
      to gable crowns a hedge.

Sermon becomes fate
when there are too many

      of them, salient becomes
      sludge when there is too
      little to consecrate the masses
      woo betide who
      woe be by-&-by wheel

  bygones-by-bygones

              out & let me go free.

      Stalwart pigeons
      in honeycombs
      strong-arm their way

      into

      smidgeons.

ABACUS

On the most exalted throne in the world,
nothing but your arse
    Montaigne

A whole lot of prattle
& beef, the suckling it were let
to reign terror on the supper table
it were. The funniest little black ting
you ever sat eyes on
& what a howlin'
& what a moanin' cooms
from the deaf dalmatian
not a dog but a right cow it were

A-twirlin' thats tail
till we's be right dizzy
plenty of work to go
a-roamin' in the streets
for idle hands there be, no use
pretendin' to be afeard mawther
curly hair be the death of virtue
the time is gettin' oover for you

If you hain't guessed by now
oo yer fader is then ya ne'er will it
right lies in his eyes, melancholia
in his spleen, frail fancy
he's a-ridin' his hobby towards ya
that as gonned you life, me pale wee iele
Kred-dhe put you
them there corsets on & bustle
Queen Mab & the laidley worm
will come a-knockin'
eft soons for the St.Vitus'
dance of the crow moon.
Mind your humours now,
be pure & clean

don't want no mudbloods
just the phrenzied
the mad & mean.

Silly puss
sluts are loathsome to fairies

STEW & YORKSHIRE PUDDING

    I

Cock-ups & crumpets
laddy wanks in his bonnet

a contribution to the stasis;
in this room of the mind
it is boring
there are pictures on the wall only seen
enough, there are books to read
only the words don't seem to please, sex
overrated unless with an animal
but the animal is satiated, is too busy
or such & such garble, while in darkness
Psyche attempts to see the face of Eros
by the light of a lamp,
                      ad nauseam.

The inflatable goat just shrivelled up
as if someone had deliberately opened
its air valve,

      the rumour spreads

like butter from yea to nay

to cupid roasting on the spit
with a hapless apple
in his mouth
      from the very origin
of the word this has been
his destiny.

It was the pink skin
like porcelain that rowed the boat
to the nether reaches.

Cupid shot an arrow in my ass
that fat foetus is jack-eyed or
didn't you know? A cock-up of monumental
proportions arming this overgrown
embryo & so the stars align
& geomancers tell of time being ripe
to catch the big fish of desiderare
before the windfucker does.

II

Germane to the groove & a close
second fret, fret just in case, hang
the jaw up to dry. The anarch & the gracioso
standing slowly outside the barber shop
holding a swell of red balloons for protection, scratch
the tegument with those thin limp claws of yore
reach terra incognita why not? Unmortise
doesn't mean the living dead now does it.

Es to es-mi to eam to AM; es-ti to ist to IS
sie to si to YES; sont to soth to SOOTHE, forsooth
aaaah! aaaaAh!

Legumes commit morthor yu!
There's no accounting for taste.
He sniffs the cork, aficionado
of agley whatsits, a new form of divination it goes

without slaying as the slaying goes, me
jinx she toot toots like a water-closet
on the blink. Sirrah!

Have you ever heard such a ting?
Begums in kagooles dying
of envy at the neighbour's new green
jalousies.
                    This things been blown
out of all proportion, up the nasal tract
& jammed itself in the bumbershoot.
Only half a queasy bracero remains,
a tenesmus is made to no avail.

The fairy she will flee if challenged
in Italian
      to straighten a pubic hair.

III

Die liebe lange Nacht floats
in partial apraxia, diagnosis: rhapsody
und wanton disbelief
in alopecia, buttons where nipples are.

BEIGNET

The window is clicking to covet this entre pass
in factus delinquent gherkins
in various stages
of hibernation,
its kind of unusual to assume
ever the worst
        only a pretence of civility
actually breeding malice & ill-will

I think she is beautiful

I see she is big

I am not blind, yet caught
between
caught & catch-it

The coxswain of the bootle bum-trinket
only one other person
                in the volatile uni-bliss
has it scratched on his jeans
chime
indigo
in chilblain thyme
what codswallop
for a crime not committed. *You're all lesbians*
                the worst possible insult hurled
by the beady blue eyed hood
of a nun with a slash
for a mouth.

En guarde ye blackheart

& I the swarthy buckler of swashes
                            lean into the wind,
all the better to hear you with my darling
                          in all your cacophagy

    out of the quagmire
          into phantasmagoria.

Watch the herd of dik-diks race to the water
as it shrivels
& the kakapo alert you
    to union sympatheico
pull your trousers up pass
the smelling salts
& the sow belly
keeping it all for yourself over there
clamming up like old drain-pipes
in the corner of the manger

That were a rough disguise
it were, no hay for the bush baby
a rumble in the bungle
      trammel up the works of say
ill-consequence & epigones
of the onslaught wired
for further entropy

The opposite of which is a
quahog on a cord
resting
on the sedulous
   declivity
      not quite immersed
         in her malachite décolletage.
So rest assured
   the shucking
     has not as yet commenced
& perplex your brow no more.

Trencherman, trencherman scry
me a river ex nihilo comes bon

>   adventure sailing on a white
>   cadillac with dorsal fins

Round & round the beautybush we go
        & all the children fattened
        on pink candy stumble
        off, green in the face swearing
        never again to go on that ride

That hit me too fast:

    Like angel-dust man too fucking fast.

If such is the case than so
it be the sky like a ragged calotte
                assures us it is dark
                at 4:30 p.m. but we know better
                all is not tref in the Hebrides.

My tutor had a monumental,

        concrete vat

in her backyard, ostensibly
for the dead bodies after
they'd been covered in yoghurt

        & spices to make a sweet treat

for the buzzards & whatever other
creatures who choose to stop by
for a free meal,
        not so quick a bite

you'd have to scale the wall
so don't go gettin' any ideas
in that pretty little 'ead of yours.

So many ingenious ways
to dispose of the dead.

        Swathed in bundles, up

in the branches of trees, shovelled

        into the ground to fraternise

with the nether world
but right dead über alles.

Organs carefully laid out in clay pots & glass jars
body stuffed with herbs & bandaged
only for some total bastard

to dig you up
& ooh & aah over
the wonder of it all.

The sky she be breedin' up
a storm she be, like the charivari
        the fälasi nurses. Looking for trehala
        in all the wrong places, with some luck

        & the blink of an eye
        Maybe it will all just go away

60 BY 120 KM ELLIPSE

Cinematic Collage

Souvent serpentine

      temples tremblement
      coucouche he swallows

a raw egg

while she watches her mother's flirtations

with the gardener

With me eyes closed & me legs
            tied by the ankles to me knees,

      don't you agree

it is a warm evening
        heavily laden with

the affectations of the age.

Beak-laden, barren cacao train

           to trepang heaven,

                  a burning glass

           to draw out the evil humours

           that cause her to wax poetic
           on all things

           imaginary.

Delay the tincture, belladonna

turning the eyes to blue

the reputation precedes the man

Oh but you do prattle, a hot battle.

        I want to know everything, everything
        you hear?

Still singing for your supper then
        but only at the best tables
        you must soft shoe it from here on now.

        Have you not noticed

how children just seem to stand there

& stare

as if possessed

        of some other knowledge.

With the wildflowers, she

        hung up to dry, she

stands still for not a moment.

Don't you love it when the grand maestro

        of all vile concoctions falls prey
        to his own devices in the end turning

        blue

        the hemlock courses
        his arteries.

'I want to be with you forever'
'Only forever?'

        Does anyone really say
        things like that.

The surah escapes
        from cold lips woven
                in Arabic for the protection
of the wearer I dare not

        state the grounds of fatwah, shimmer

With patriarchy,
        'It's the ward man's wind,'

the tatterdemalion tells of, bereft of,

        emoticons all will us to the berth

of fervour bled onto the willows.

Gullet sheets moan hard & extend
                trespasses to the untoward & mild

at ease only death opens their ears

        to logos ohm see, unsee

the flight of fallacy

        & dull conviction.

Tall, pale & interesting, he bore
the countenance of a body surfer afloat
        in the bog altricial & alight
with the storm-watch
           of the blind worm feeble a fllial fiddle

Get thee to a nunnery

A male excursion no doubt

grasping

for all manner of nurses & natural fact
           marry nuncle a marimba survives
           the overcast bereavement of a kind
           of soulless body.

The holy hour arrives
when the last cigarette ingratiates itself

           to the senses, fat man in a

           slim chance suit how now

a visit come visit & rage.

Trench mouth your eohippus
           waits in the eaves for you
           to put down the trough
           of feed but before you leave

Let's have a go
at the merry thought

once & for all

to see whose
            wishes

may in fact
    come true

VALHALLA

I

Sufferin' jehosaphats
jumpin' snakeskin
jambalaya & the crow leapt
over the wickets, shake a leg & miss
the boat anyway curses!

De bread she is de spoiled
again, gotta cut off the green bits
to make toast for tea & dare say
we something as passé as
je ne sais quoi & it's off wid her head
just for sport like the Norman
who hunts peacocks.

Bad business this, I tell you
clean out of my head it's gone
now where was I? Ah yes horticulture
& torture together again like old enemies
who have kissed & made up, that rings a bell

Won't catch me potting a goddamn thing
& what of a person with no thumbs at all
neither green nor black, just void
& the world becomes your mussel
except you loathe mussels

With the same grand passion that you long
for that bloody man tenaciously
but somehow, somehow
it always seems wrong.

There is not a scratch of purity
in the emotion, not a thimble's worth
& for the life of you
you just can't figure it out like most things,

in the middle of the night
when figuring outings are made.

II

Sufferance, a fine line that shiver me
timbre, miss or hit a glistening
dangerous chit circa through the ages
of gall & gumption, not lacking
in the least bit.

Sie ist meine Schwester
& I think she's ugly.
Better you than me
on occasion is felt joie
in a safely guarded, controlled
environment they like to tell us
how the water's running out.
What did they think?
That it wouldn't?

& the *bijli*
that is in short supply apparently
this comes as no shock
Hephaestus is no human ally
Ra signed no contract
to provide power to Earth

Pachamama is rent
asunder, at this juncture
The sea is going to become
one cataclysmic cesspool
we do away with anyone
who knows the ways
of the land right off the bat.

Creatures doomed
to state the obvious
what a plight for
pillocks!

III

Bedknobs & bromide
on the nightstand is the Grimoire
a sweet dream for the glazed-eyed.
I long for the lekjas to appear again
in all his vainglory so I can pull
at his robes & denounce him
for the imposter that he is, like a scream
in an anechoic chamber
suspended, I pretend
to sleep with Odin.

AFTERWORD
Sascha Aurora Akhtar

I etch my own face upon my wicked flesh.
I am my own devastating god.
    Rachel McKibbens

The pressure to write something smashing on the occasion of one's own work being exhumed from the necropolis of poetic utterances has been too great for me. After all, I have been saying a great deal during the seventeen years since the publication of this manuscript. And many have heard me. This has been a comfort. When this book came out, I felt abysmally unheard. In fact, it is because I have never stopped writing, never stopped performing, that this book is being brought back onto the stage. Encore! Encore! Am I ready? I can't say for sure. I will be ready. I tried reading some poems at a Salon the other day, they felt odd in my mouth, yet so familiar. Thick boughs to chew on. Melded vines. The roots though, the roots, as the roots of language, all language still live in my body. How can they not?

    I have been missing Bernadette Mayer. I know she would be happy to know about the reincarnation of the *Grimoire*. I have said it before: she is the reason this book ever left the machine it was written on. Well, Sophie too. Sophia, the Wise and Beautiful. Bernadette's daughter. My sister from this other mother, who is my poetry mother. You see, I never knew anything about Bernadette. I was a kid at college, who reached the age of eighteen not knowing very much about Western culture. Literature. Art. Certainly not contemporary culture. It seemed everyone knew who Sophie's Mom 'was'. Sophie was my mate! I actually went to uni to pursue my passion of film and analogue photography. I wrote my first poem at the age of eight and before that I had always filled diaries with writing. Writing was just what I did. I never centred it as my 'thing'. In fact, when I attempted to join Creative Writing workshops, I was pretty much told I was shit. I know now, they just hadn't read anything like it yet, certainly not from a non-White woman. Mary Oliver rejected me from her poetry workshop. In your twenties, things like this hit hard. There were other unkind white poets along the way too. It was a few years after I graduated, 2001 I believe, when Sophie gave me her Mom's book. It was Midwinter Day and Sophie said, 'Hey this my Mom's book. Maybe you want to read it.' So I did.

An odd thing. I read it all in one sitting. That was my first experience of contemporary poetry. What occurred next? I sat down and wrote a book all in one sitting. It has never been published!

I gave the book to Sophia. I had titled it *Golum* and I said 'Maybe your Mom will like this.' Bernadette delighted in receiving books. It was her great joy and so she happily received it and read it. She said she loved it and invited me to read at what I lovingly call 'The Great Anti-Independence Day Lake TsatsaWassa Convention'. Every year, Bernadette and Phil invited their mates to come and read at their place in Upstate New York on 5 July. I was invited to share too.

Who were her mates? Well, that was how I came to know Michael Gizzi, a maverick, musician and cool guy. Simon Pettet. Peter Gizzi. I think Brenda Coultis was there. There were others too. I think not knowing who any of them 'were' was probably helpful. I remember feeling completely insane and awkward and anxious. However, they all welcomed me and seemed to appreciate my work. This is how I became the creature I am.

Bernadette continued to be a sort of guide. I sent her everything I wrote. She read it and always loved it. So much was occurring in my personal life. I was navigating immigration, questions of home – I was lost, very lost. Drugs were a feature. Poverty was a feature. But these were not the things she was privy to.

I cannot say how exactly the *Grimoire* came about. I remember this incredible black hat, like a top hat but fashioned of velvet, soft and lush. I remember something growing in my head. I remember deciding I was going to 'write a book'. The hat was important to the book. I remember my good friend, an environmental scientist, was living in the apartment across, with some physicists. She presented me with an American Heritage Dictionary. As a child, I used to read dictionaries. It was great fun. Neither I nor my friend could have known just how important this dictionary would prove to be, setting me off on a journey through the roots of the English language and further in all languages. The scientists across the hall would knock on my door and find me in my hat, with a mad look in my eyes. They would ask if I wanted to come round for a beer and some food. I would decline. Catherine would look at my hat and say 'Ooookay Sascha'.

I sat down every day for a month and a half and wrote it. When it was done, it went straight to Bernadette. I had no understanding of what I had written. Everything felt so mysterious. What did it mean?

What did I mean? What were these poems? I had no idea. I had become obsessed with the idea of primordial language and the Tower of Babel. Bakhtin had fascinated me in terms of content, and I was enamoured with Deleuze & Guattari's rhizome model as an approach to forms.

I cannot write another book in this foreword. Not even an essay. This is meant to enhance your experience. The *Grimoire* paved the way for everything. I sent it out to a random online literary magazine called *Annetna Nepo*. The editor, Philip John Usher, told me it was an anagram for Open Antenna. I didn't know he was at Harvard at the time or would invite me to read at a poetry reading series there. I sent ten pages of the unpublished *Grimoire* to a writing programme. It got me a place on an M.F.A and a full fellowship.

It wasn't until six years later and a relocation to the UK – after being told by a UK editor that it was 'verbal vomit', after being asked 'What are these? Dictionary poems?' by someone who is now a 'prestigious poet', after suffering at the hands of The White Boys Club of poetry in an academic setting – that the book was finally published by Salt Publishing.

When I moved to the UK, I emailed a poet whose website I had found. Somehow, without meeting, and via email only, we both arrived at the conclusion that we were fed up with the 'poetry scene' and the Dead White Man phenomenon, and decided to set up a reading series of our own. By this time, I had sent the poet my manuscript. I thought he would think I was crazy. It turns out he was the best reader the best reader I could have asked for at the time. No, really. The poetics that he was involved with spoke to mine. We were trying to decide on a name for the reading series. And he said, 'Why not call it La Langoustine Est Morte?' A line from the very first poem in the book! I refused. It felt embarrassing, but his belief in my words prevailed. He sent the book to his publisher. Even after I had refused that too! Such was the state of my belief in myself after exposing myself to academia. Who was this poet? It was Anthony Joseph.

All of the above came to pass: the reading series, which a fair few readers will know and remember. The book itself... And the magic of the *Grimoire* didn't stop there. Had it not been for the subsequent *Grimoire* book launch, some years after, I may never have returned to the UK or continued my life here. In between the book being prepared for publishing and the book being launched, I had my personal life crash and burn yet again, and was in a state of deep grief in Pakistan

– the place I left at the age of eighteen.

    I find myself deeply grateful for it, and now on the eve of its re-emergence as I have looked back and pondered all this and more, I realise that all I have been teaching regarding magical praxis and poetry, and all that I have come to see poetry as – an agent of the deep unknown, a way to alchemize and transform – may yet be truer than I imagined at the time. And so I send this work of mine out to pound the pavement again.

    Sascha Aurora Akhtar
    17 July 2024
    London

ACKNOWLEDGEMENTS

The Author acknowledges the unseen: the ancestors who have passed and the wider circle of the dead psychic workers. I wish to use this acknowledgement space to acknowledge the abject rotting failure of societies built only on individualistic concerns fuelled by violence towards the collective. Therefore, I cannot in good faith present this artefact, this documentation of praxis except in the Buddhist sense, which always includes the collective: by the power and truth of this practice, may all sentient beings possess happiness and the causes of happiness. May all sentient beings be free of suffering and the causes of suffering and live in the great equanimity devoid of suffering. I acknowledge, too, the fire of all fires. All the waters. The earth below and the air we all breathe and I send these acknowledgements off to the skies we share. May my sweet blossom Sakura find these words in some iteration of the future and know and know her love means everything to me.

Sascha Aurora Akhtar has published seven collections of poetry. Her first short story collection, *Of Necessity And Wanting*, was shortlisted for the UBL Prize for Literary Excellence in 2023. Akhtar translated *Belles-Lettres: Writings of Hijab Imtiaz Ali*, the first translation of Ali's 'Adab-e-Zareen', which was published by Oxford University Press in 2023. *Belles-Lettres* received an Honourable Mention for the 2024 A.K. Ramanujan Prize for book translations from South Asian languages into English, awarded by the Association for Asian Studies. A third-generation psychic in the Lancashire lineage, Akhtar studied in Pakistan and at Bennington College, Vermont, and the University of Amherst, Massachusetts.

Akhtar performs internationally; highlights include the Emirates Festival of Literature, Poetry Wales and Rotterdam Poetry Festival. She is a Creative Writing lecturer at the University of Greenwich and has been facilitating the melding of magical praxis and writing at the Poetry School, London, since 2019, cultivating an international cohort of practitioners.

ABOUT PROTOTYPE

poetry / prose / interdisciplinary projects / anthologies

Creating new possibilities in the publishing of fiction and poetry through a flexible, interdisciplinary approach and the production of unique and beautiful books.

Prototype is an independent publisher working across genres and disciplines, committed to discovering and sharing work that exists outside the mainstream.

Each publication is unique in its form and presentation, and the aesthetic of each object is considered critical to its production.

Prototype strives to increase audiences for experimental writing, as the home for writers and artists whose work requires a creative vision not offered by mainstream literary publishers.

In its current, evolving form, Prototype consists of 4 strands of publications:

(type 1 — poetry)
(type 2 — prose)
(type 3 — interdisciplinary projects)
(type 4 — anthologies) including an annual anthology of new work, *PROTOTYPE*.

The Grimoire of Grimalkin by Sascha Aurora Akhtar
Published by Prototype in 2024

The right of Sascha Aurora Akhtar to be identified as author of this work has been asserted in accordance with Section 77 of the UK Copyright, Designs and Patents Act 1988.

Copyright © Sascha Aurora Akhtar 2024
All rights reserved

Originally published by Salt Publishing in 2007

No part of this publication may be reproduced, stored in a retrieval system, or transmitted, in any form or by any means, electronic, mechanical, photocopying, recording or otherwise, without the prior permission of the publishers. A CIP record for this book is available from the British Library.

Design by Matthew Stuart & Andrew Walsh-Lsiter
(Traven T. Croves)
Typeset in Laurier (Beta) by Seb Mclauchlan
Printed in the UK by Bell & Bain Ltd, Glasgow

The illustration of the author as a cat, by Sally Kemp, originally appeared in Kiran Toor's article 'Open Conduit: Sascha Akhtar's *The Grimoire of Grimalkin*', published in the October 2008 issue of *The London Magazine*. Every effort has been made to contact the original artist.

ISBN 978-1-913513-40-5

( ) (   ) p   prototype

(type 1 – poetry)
www.prototypepublishing.co.uk
@prototypepubs

prototype publishing
71 oriel road
london e9 5sg
uk

Besides an inveterate love of language which makes you write 'her malachite décolletage', whatever else you need to be a good poet is here. It could be sounds. Come right in; don't step gently then.
    Bernadette Mayer

On reading *The Grimoire of Grimalkin*, it's clear that Sascha Aurora Akhtar is a language-diviner, her poems conjured from 'the galaxy of lingual acrobatics.' Akhtar's poems, which are like nobody else's, are gobsmacking, magical. This work casts a wild, incantatory music that beguiles both ear and tongue.
    Sylvia Legris

Sascha Akhtar repels ghosts with this text and liberates the word from the burden of meaning. These poems are spells and sonorous soundings that have the power to frighten, seduce or enchant. Akhtar aspires to magic. This is a timeless and vital collection from a poet willing to transcend the liminal.
    Anthony Joseph

The sign of visionary poetics is that the vision remains ever-prescient, practically omniscient, no matter when. *The Grimoire of Grimalkin* again reminds us that each word's unending algal mitosis coincides with a grand carnival to which everyone's invited, thus requiring a poet who can trim and tie back the dark wood and hand-remove pests one by one, so buds can reform on branches over a doorway unseen until right then. Sascha Aurora Akhtar's book is time*less*space. Her voices were near to us, nearer now with this new release – le femmine balbe, le serene, who speak over those epic men attempting to mime them or chime with them. Akhtar's voices say: Eat your heart out, it's mine, anyway, my dear reader, dearie me, mon frère, ma soeur, why don't you come in.
    Kimberly Campanello

The Grimoire of Grimalkin reads like a weave of lexical magic. So much corpsing rising and falling. A sly evil turning on the head of a charged intonal hex. Herein lies a poetry as precipitous as it is substantial, movement and cathexis. Ultimately leaving language to become orphaned from its sign. Casted beyond the reaches of any linguistic mastery over its braided, interpolated symbolism under the generative idiom of Sacha Ahktar's inexhaustible poetic registers giving weight and force to the inexpressible.
    James Goodwin

We read rage here – a necessary catalyst for transforming and preserving Akhtar's geographies of otherness, both in the body and in society. Such rage extends to environmental concerns, as she critiques the destruction and toxicity of our worlds. *The Grimoire of Grimalkin* becomes a reflection of Akhtar's anger with both inner and outer environmental degradation, transcending specific locations to encompass a universal critique of human, animal, and plant conditions.
    Ghazal Mosadeq